The
Green
Witch's
ORACLE
DECK

of Natural Magic

ARIN MURPHY-HISCOCK
AUTHOR OF **The Green Witch**

ILLUSTRATED BY SARA RICHARD

ADAMS MEDIA
New York London Toronto Sydney New Delhi

Adams Media
An Imprint of Simon
& Schuster, Inc.
100 Technology Center Drive
Stoughton, Massachusetts
02072

Copyright © 2023 by
Simon & Schuster, Inc.

First Adams Media trade
paperback edition December
2023

ADAMS MEDIA and colophon
are registered trademarks of
Simon & Schuster, Inc.

For information about special
discounts for bulk purchases,
please contact Simon &
Schuster Special Sales at
1-866-506-1949 or business@
simonandschuster.com.

The Simon & Schuster Speakers
Bureau can bring authors
to your live event. For more
information or to book an
event, contact the Simon
& Schuster Speakers Bureau
at 1-866-248-3049 or
visit our website at
www.simonspeakers.com.

Interior design by Priscilla Yuen
Illustrations by Sara Richard
Interior images © 123RF/
KATSUMI MUROUCHI;
Getty Images/kenny371;
Simon & Schuster, Inc.

Manufactured in China

10 9 8 7 6 5

ISBN 978-1-5072-2113-6

Contents

PART 3

THE CARDS AND HOW TO INTERPRET THEM • 27

Introduction

THE PATH OF GREEN WITCHCRAFT is deeply personal. It is built on your individual connection to the natural world and its many gifts. As an herbalist, healer, and naturalist, you nourish and encourage this connection by seeking guidance from nature, relying on the power of natural elements to improve your physical well-being, your spirit, and the environment. *The Green Witch's Oracle Deck* was created to help you on this journey.

Whether you are looking to strengthen your connection to nature, enhance your intuition, confront a situation that has been troubling you, or simply open communication between yourself and the natural world, *The Green Witch's Oracle Deck* provides everything you need to incorporate oracle cards in your practice.

While anyone can consult this magical deck, it is uniquely suited for green witch practitioners. It draws from the symbols, actions, and concepts closely associated with green witchcraft, and through these symbols seeks to help you navigate the various situations in your own life. The focus of the fifty cards ranges from stones, insects, and seasons, to plants, trees, and garden tools—each one holds a special message to help you evaluate and face any challenges you encounter, like a personal guide designed just for you.

What makes this deck so special is that each card also includes a reflective question grounded in green magic to help you really consider your emotions, motives, and potential solutions to any issues. This is your moment to delve deeply into your spirit to find the answer you need. Green witchcraft is fluid, so feel at liberty to explore meanings, create connections between cards, and free-associate during your readings—whatever makes you feel closest to your oracle deck. This booklet will also explain how to prepare yourself for a reading, pose specific questions, use spreads effectively, and interpret the messages the cards are sending you.

The Green Witch's Oracle Deck is here to provide advice rooted in the natural world. Be it herb, stone, plant, tool, or physical action, everything has wisdom to impart. All you need to do is reflect on it to discover how you can weave that wisdom into your life.

PART 1

UNDERSTANDING YOUR GREEN WITCH'S ORACLE DECK

The Green Witch's Oracle Deck draws inspiration from the many elements found in the natural world. Green witchcraft teaches you that every detail in nature has meaning and purpose, and this deck will help you integrate that message into your practice. The following chapter offers information on what you can learn from this deck, how you can use it, and how you can better understand its connections to your magical and/or spiritual practice.

← CHAPTER 1 →
Oracle Deck Basics

There are many ways *The Green Witch's Oracle Deck* can be used to encourage your intuitive and spiritual practices. As you learn more about these cards and yourself, you can build a relationship with this deck that feels most authentic and matched to your needs. The symbols of green witchcraft found in this deck are the basic parts of your environment—they are the herbs, stones, plants, seasons, flowers, trees, and tools that lay the foundation for life. Communing with them offers a chance to unleash your organic power—the untamed energy that grows from the spirit/nature connection.

Getting to Know Your Green Witch's Oracle Deck

Oracle decks are a free-form divination tool that you can adapt to your needs and wants. Instead of having a set series of meanings for the cards, as a tarot deck often does, an oracle deck uses associations to encourage you to interpret the card(s) freely. In Part 3 of this booklet, you will find explanations of each card and its meaning, key information about the symbol or action related to the card, what the card could potentially be telling you to consider, and a question for you to contemplate in connection with the overall message of the card and how it may apply to your life.

Main Uses of This Deck

The two main reasons for using *The Green Witch's Oracle Deck* are for divination and for developing your intuition; both can be useful when you are seeking answers to major questions. Divination helps you gain insight or information about something, while intuition is the sense that guides you without the need for conscious reasoning or obvious or immediate proof. Together, these concepts can help you explore information available to you that might not be accessible through more logic-driven means.

Divination

Divination allows you to tap into information that you might not otherwise pick up—information that can offer insight into yourself and the world around you. Figuring out the best way to frame a question to your cards can be tricky sometimes. If you're too specific (for example, asking "What day is going to be the best day to ask for a raise next week?"), your oracle deck may not be able to provide a precise answer. To get the most benefit from your deck, stick to open-ended questions (for example, "What should I keep in mind when I ask for a raise?").

Here are some examples of questions you might want to ask your deck:

✦ *What message does the natural world have for me today?*
✦ *What obstacles are facing me?*
✦ *What do I need to watch out for or pay attention to?*
✦ *How can I enrich my green witchcraft practice?*

The more energy you put into honing your divination skills, the closer you will get to formulating the most beneficial questions.

Developing Your Intuition

Intuition serves an important role in how you approach the cards you've drawn when doing an oracle reading. Before you check the meaning of the cards you've drawn in Part 3 of this booklet, consider asking yourself the following questions, which can help bring the card's true meaning for you into light:

✦ *How do I interpret the card?*
✦ *What does the art make me think of?*
✦ *What role does the item or action play in my life?*
✦ *What's my first overall response to the card?*

While divination and developing intuition are the dominant uses for this deck, green witchcraft is a flexible practice that is self-designed to support you in various parts of your life, so if you would like to use this deck in other ways (spellwork, rituals, meditation), follow your heart.

PART 2

Working with the Deck

Understanding how to best prepare your deck (and yourself) for a reading is very important when using any divination tool, including oracle cards. This part will explore different ways to properly approach oracle readings.

CHAPTER 2

Preparing Your Deck
for Readings

It's important to remember that you are working *with* your oracle deck; it is not working *for* you. Your energy and the energy of the cards will interact to create the reading. That's why an oracle deck should be cleansed, dedicated, and attuned to your energy before you begin using it. With a clear deck you can imprint your own energy so it better serves you during your readings.

Cleansing and Dedicating Your Deck

The first step in preparing your deck for your first reading is cleansing it of any previous energy. Do this by spreading out the cards in the sunlight or moonlight for as long as you feel it necessary; it could be a day or night or a full lunar month. Once your deck has been cleansed, it is time to cleanse your space. There are many options to cleanse your space, but one of the easiest employed in green witch-craft includes using your actual household broom to sweep your floors while visualizing the removal of stale energy.

Blessing Your Deck

With a clear deck and space, you are now ready to bless and dedicate your deck so it will better respond to you and your energy.

GREEN WITCH'S ORACLE DECK BLESSING

WHAT YOU NEED:
+ *Green Witch's Oracle Deck*
+ *Your preferred blessing incense (sandalwood is a good choice)*
+ *Censer or a vessel made specifically for burning incense*
+ *1 small white candle (such as a tea light)*
+ *Matches or lighter*
+ *Small bowl of salt*
+ *Small bowl of water*

WHAT TO DO:
1 Lay the deck in the center of your workspace.
2 Place the incense in the censer and light it.
3 Light the candle.
4 Above the upper left corner of the deck, place the bowl of salt. Above the upper right corner, place the censer. At the lower right corner, place the candle. At the lower left corner, place the bowl of water.

5 Speak your intention:

> *I ask the four elements to be present*
> *as I bless this oracle deck,*
> *and dedicate it to my use as I follow*
> *the path of the green witch.*

6 Hold your hand above the bowl of salt and say:

> *Earth, bless this deck with wisdom.*

7 Waft the incense smoke over the deck with your hand and say:

> *Air, bless this deck with clear communication.*

8 Hold your hand around the candle and say:

> *Fire, bless this deck with inspiration.*

9 Hold your hand above the bowl of water and say:

> *Water, bless this deck with insight.*

10 Hold the deck in your hands and close your eyes. Imagine your energy growing like blue tendrils out of your palms and flowing into the oracle deck. Next, visualize pale green energy tendrils growing out of the deck, intertwining with yours. Allow the energies to mingle. At some point during this process, you should feel a strong connection build between you and your deck.

Attuning to Your Deck

Attuning to your deck allows you to form a closer relationship with each card in the deck and with the deck as a whole. The best way to attune to your deck is to go through the deck one card at a time, exploring the illustration. How does it make you feel? What associated images or ideas does it evoke? What does the card's subject mean to you? Record your personal interpretation of the card.

Next, read through Part 3 of this booklet and consider the ideas and associations written for each card. Are they similar to your interpretation? Do they contradict in some way? If so, always rely on your interpretation of the card's subject over that of the booklet.

Deck Maintenance and Storage

Your preferences for handling and sharing your oracle cards will determine how you store and care for the deck. Will you allow other people to handle the cards? If so, your oracle deck will pick up energy from being in emotional situations, being handled by different people, and being read in different environments. Will you cleanse the deck regularly, or accept that energy as part of the deck's purpose?

How you store your oracle deck is entirely up to you. Most green witches like to have their deck protected in some way from casual touch. You can wrap your deck in a square of natural cloth such as cotton, linen, or silk. You can keep it in a wooden box or a bag. You can store it with a protective sachet of herbs or stones. Whatever fits into your worldview and practice best is fine!

CHAPTER 3

How to Read Oracle Cards

This chapter explores potential issues you may encounter when getting ready for a reading, suggestions for properly executing a reading, and step-by-step instructions for using the oracle deck during a reading.

When and Where to Do Your Reading

You can do a reading with this deck whenever you like. While there are no set requirements regarding when to do a reading, some factors may influence your results. For example, you can choose the time according to what you want from the reading. If you want to hold an idea in your mind as you fall asleep to allow your subconscious to work on it as you dream, pull a card just before bed.

You can also consult a moon sign schedule to see when the moon is passing through a zodiac sign that resonates with your goal, and schedule a reading for that time, or you can consult a planetary hours schedule and time a reading for the hour of whatever planet you feel drawn to.

Where you do your reading depends on where you feel most comfortable and open. Do you have a sacred place, inside or outside? That is usually ideal, as the energy will be familiar and keyed to yours.

Creating a Divination Routine

It is important to note that your state of mind can have a huge effect on your reading. The clearer and more open you are, the more the cards will give you. To help you get into the headspace most conducive to a reading, it may help to write and use a personalized invocation/declaration to set intention before each reading. This can be the common step before every reading, no matter how complex.

Additionally, using a familiar set of items can further support your experience. A specific cloth to lay the cards on not only protects them from dirt on whatever surface you're about to work on, but it can serve as a key object to help you slip into a focused mental state before a reading.

Performing a Reading

Once you have chosen the time and place for your reading and completed your prereading preparation routine, you're ready to start pulling cards. The following instructions will help guide you in this process.

Forming Your Question

You can choose your layout ahead of time, or wing it. Take some time to think about your question and make it as clear as you can. It's also possible to do a reading without a specific question, as a kind of insight for general life guidance, by simply clearing your mind and asking the deck what you need to know right now. Close your eyes and take three deep breaths.

Drawing Your Card

Hold the question or issue in your mind while shuffling the cards calmly. If, as you're shuffling, cards fall out, you can pick them up and shuffle them right back in, you can put them to the side without looking at them and use them as clarifying cards later, or you can use them as the first cards in the layout. When you are done shuffling, hold the deck in your hands. Pose your question silently or aloud.

Choose your card (or cards). This can be any card in the deck—you can pull the one on top or any card from any place in the deck. You can cut the deck and pull from the middle somewhere. Or you can divide the deck into the number of stacks that matches the number of cards called for in the layout, then take the top card of each stack and place them in the pattern indicated by the layout of the spread.

Interpret Your Reading

Now start looking for deeper connections. For a one-card draw, ask yourself what parallels you see between the card's meaning and your life. For a spread, consider if the items or actions are associated in some way. Clarifying cards can be pulled if, after your layout is done and you've interpreted everything as far as you can, you still feel like something isn't clear or complete. Draw one or more card(s) and place them by the card(s) you feel need further explanation.

Recording Your Reading

Keeping a record of your readings will help you draw connections not only between cards, but between major themes uncovered in your readings. The record of your reading doesn't have to be extensive. At the very least, though, you should include the date and time, what cards were involved, and your initial thoughts about it and/or an interpretation. Additionally, you should make note of any cards that fell out of the deck while you were shuffling or any clarification cards you pulled.

— CHAPTER 4 —
Oracle Card Spreads

This chapter provides you with ideas for card spreads that you can use with *The Green Witch's Oracle Deck*. In a spread, each card has a specific position assigned to it. The card laid in that position offers insight into that specific area. Trust your energy and the energy of your cards.

A note about card placement: When you draw a card, you can lay it face up right away, or if you prefer, you can draw and place all the cards of the spread face down, then either turn them all over and do your interpretation, or turn them over one by one.

ONE-CARD SPREAD ✦ Quick Connection

A simple one-card draw is good for the green witch looking for quick guidance from the natural world. It is a wonderful way to form a fast connection to nature that you can nourish until your next reading. Remember to trust that the universe is bringing you this card for a reason. Focus on one question, shuffle the deck, and draw a single card.

THREE-CARD SPREAD ✦ The Green Witch's Past, Present, and Future

This version of the three-card spread explores areas of your life that need to be addressed in different ways. Draw and lay out the cards according to your preference, then consider how that card provides answers to the following questions:

CARD 1: What do I need to sow in order to lay good foundations for a future project?

CARD 2: What in my life requires tending to in order to maximize success in the future?

CARD 3: What in my life has come to the point where it needs to be concluded and harvested?

FIVE-CARD SPREAD ✦ The Elements

This five-card spread uses the four classical elements and a fifth card, representing spirit, to help you explore a particular issue. Air, earth, fire, and water, and the fifth element, spirit, can offer deep wisdom.

Starting from the upper left corner of your workspace and moving clockwise, lay down four cards in an open square. In the center of the square, lay a fifth card.

CARD 1 (upper left): *Earth.* What are the effects of this issue on my body and physical state?

CARD 2 (upper right): *Air.* What are the effects of this issue on my mind and mental state?

CARD 3 (lower right): *Fire.* What are the effects of this issue on others?

CARD 4 (lower left): *Water.* What are the effects of this issue on my emotional well-being?

CARD 5 (center): *Spirit.* What are the effects of this issue on my spiritual well-being?

SIX-CARD SPREAD ✦ The Tree

This six-card spread looks at the roots, manifestation, and solution for your situation or problem. Trees form the backbone of the green witch's practice. The roots of a tree can reach deep into the earth for stability and for nourishment. Its branches reach high into the sky so that the leaves of the tree may absorb as much sunlight as possible and further nourish the tree. Place the cards in the following order, as per the illustrated layout:

CARD 1: The root of the problem.
CARD 2: The trunk, where the problem is.
CARD 3: The heart of the problem.
CARD 4: Where you can draw strength and seek solutions.
CARD 5: Help will come from this area unasked.
CARD 6: Areas and ideas to be open to in order to advance through the problem.

NINE-CARD SPREAD + The Garden Gate

A gate is a symbol of liminality or boundary, moving from one place to another. Think of the gate to your green witch's garden—it separates energy and purpose. This nine-card spread will help you understand a problem by looking at its source, current expression, effects, and future path so that you can step past it.

Lay seven cards in an arch shape, following the 1–7 order as indicated here. The space within the arch should be wide enough for a card.

CARDS 1 and 2: The foundations of the problem.
CARDS 3 and 4: How the problem manifests now.
CARDS 5 and 6: How the problem affects your life.
CARD 7: How you react to the problem.

Then draw two more cards, placing them in the center of the arch.

CARD 8: Laid in the center of the arch, to be the lock; this card represents the core of the obstacle.

CARD 9: Laid horizontally across the lock card, to be the key; this card represents what will help you work through the challenge and get to the other side of the situation.

TWELVE-CARD SPREAD ✦ Wheel of the Year

The Wheel of the Year spread will help you see what the coming year has in store for you. While everything in nature is cyclical, such as the seasons and the moon phases, each year brings with it a variation in purpose. This spread can help illuminate what you should focus on in the coming year, challenges that may come up, and what energies you may encounter.

CARD 1: Month 1
CARD 2: Month 2
CARD 3: Month 3
CARD 4: Month 4
CARD 5: Month 5
CARD 6: Month 6

CARD 7: Month 7
CARD 8: Month 8
CARD 9: Month 9
CARD 10: Month 10
CARD 11: Month 11
CARD 12: Month 12

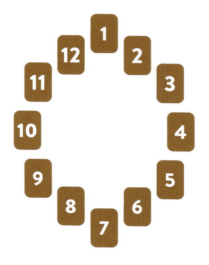

PART 3

The Cards and How to Interpret Them

The cards in this deck are based on the tenets of green magic: seasons, stages of plant growth, garden tools and magical tools (which can be the same things in green witchcraft), herbs, stones, and garden creatures. Each card has been selected according to its symbolism and how it can function in a green witch's practice and development. Some of the cards are based on actions or more abstract concepts, such as *preserve* or *tend*. These concepts have their own energy and application within the natural cycle. Using both abstracts and physical objects in an oracle deck allows your reading to be multifac-eted, encouraging you to pay attention to action as well as objects in your daily life.

BROOM

Energy clearing, freshening

BROOM

ENERGY CLEARING, FRESHENING

CARD MEANING: The Broom card reminds you to clear away any outdated and stale energy in your life that is leaving you feeling stuck. It is time to brush away musty emotions and patterns. On a practical level, a broom clears away physical crumbs, dirt, and dust, which allows you a tidy space, so energy flows more smoothly. Without any debris in your way, your mind and magic will function more efficiently.

With intention, use the broom to stir up stale energy, sweep away negative or unsupportive energy, and create a space that is ready for your individual needs. You can do this physically, with an actual broom and a quick cleansing of your magical space, or mentally, by envisioning what doesn't serve you being swept away.

REFLECTION

What areas of your life need to be straightened up, dusted off, and refreshed?

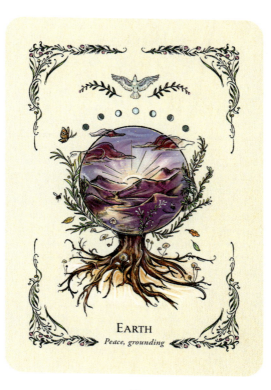

EARTH

Peace, grounding

EARTH

PEACE, GROUNDING

CARD MEANING: The Earth card offers a moment of reflection and connection. You may be losing yourself and becoming too focused on work, schedules, and to-do lists. Sometimes you don't realize how far you've strayed from your relationship with nature and its calming energy. Even those of us who work with nature daily can sometimes get set in our ways and become complacent. This card is a reminder to consciously renew your connection with nature and listen to what the natural world has to say.

Take a step back and breathe, giving yourself space to find balance. Clear your mind and open it to the communication of nature. Let its energy soothe and revitalize you as you ground yourself in the earth.

REFLECTION

Do you need to reboot your connection to nature, or maybe help someone else to connect to nature?

31

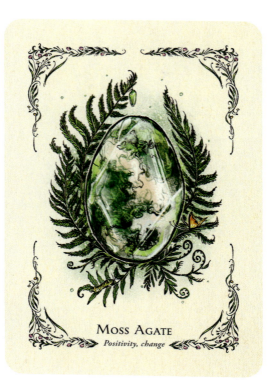

Moss Agate

Positivity, change

MOSS AGATE

POSITIVITY, CHANGE

CARD MEANING: Change can be daunting. The Moss Agate card reminds you that stasis, while comfortable, denies you the growth and development that your spirit needs to evolve. Moss agate offers you the foundation, or a safe space, to explore and plan for the future.

You are holding back from change because you feel unprepared. Moss agate can help. Moss agate attracts positive energy, a boon when you are uncertain about shifts and transformations in life. Call on this stone to help set good foundations and prepare yourself for future change, or simply when you crave emotional balance.

REFLECTION

Is there an upcoming change that you have been avoiding that you need to make peace with?

SAGE

Wisdom, purification, harmony

SAGE

WISDOM, PURIFICATION, HARMONY

CARD MEANING: Sage is a wise herb. It reassures you that you are grounded and stable, and that the wisdom you need is easily accessible if you look in the right place. The Sage card reminds you that insight can appear from unlikely sources. Being in harmony with your environment allows you to receive messages and act on them more easily than if you are living in discord. Listening can bring balance, and purification can remove obstacles that further cloud that exchange of information and communication.

Remember that what may not make sense now might fall into place later. Don't be so quick to dismiss advice that doesn't make sense immediately. Remain open and wisdom will come to you.

REFLECTION

How can you help to facilitate the communication of wisdom from your surroundings?

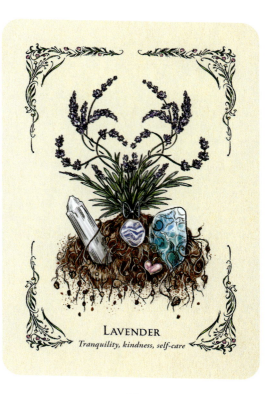

LAVENDER

Tranquility, kindness, self-care

LAVENDER

TRANQUILITY, KINDNESS, SELF-CARE

CARD MEANING: Lavender is a popular green witchcraft herb, often associated with peace, tranquility, rest, and relaxation. Its stress-relieving properties make it the perfect herb to use in various self-care applications, such as in a bath or essential oil.

Take a moment to consider whether you've been kind enough to yourself lately. The Lavender card is a great reminder to take stock of how you treat yourself. Remember that kindness comes in many forms. You may have been critical of yourself or your body lately. Maybe you have been driving yourself too hard without eating or sleeping properly. Take a moment for yourself to restore your equilibrium. This is a great time to re-examine your life to see what changes you could make to facilitate less stress in general.

REFLECTION

What area of your life needs kindness right now?

POTION

Invigoration, empowerment

POTION

INVIGORATION, EMPOWERMENT

CARD MEANING: The Potion card tells you that a small infusion of intention, even just a drop, can invigorate you and get you back on track if you are feeling out of control. Any act done with intention can stimulate forward momentum.

Choosing to empower yourself with a small gesture of concentrated magic can refresh you enough to galvanize your motivation. This may be as simple as casting a basic spell or meditating in nature. Not every action needs to be huge, and not every change is immediate and sweeping. Don't discount the magic that a tiny gesture or moment can create. Just a small drop will do.

REFLECTION

What energizes you on a daily basis?

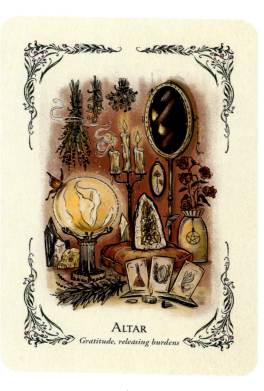

ALTAR

Gratitude, releasing burdens

ALTAR

GRATITUDE, RELEASING BURDENS

CARD MEANING: It is important to make time and space for connecting with Spirit. In that space, look into your heart for truths. The Altar card can help you reflect on your blessings and what you need to express gratitude for.

Conversely, look inside for the truth about your challenges. There may be something you need to release to the universe in order to grow and flourish, or a burden you need to surrender so that you can move forward. The Altar can help. Take stock of what you are grateful for. Think about what you can offer nature or Spirit to share your blessings.

REFLECTION

What isn't serving you and can be released into the universe for you to move on?

CAULDRON

Creation, opportunity, caring

CAULDRON

CREATION, OPPORTUNITY, CARING

CARD MEANING: Self-transformation, one of the central goals of witchcraft, can be intimidating. The Cauldron card reassures you that brewing change is a chance to create new opportunities for yourself as well as those around you. This can be as simple as adopting a fresh outlook.

The cauldron encourages you to think creatively and to try combining things that may not seem to work together at first glance to solve a problem.

The cauldron is also a symbol of nourishing yourself and others. Caring for those around you is an enriching pursuit for all involved.

REFLECTION

Are you avoiding brainstorming different solutions when faced with a problem?

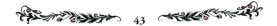

MOTH

Mystery, concealment, illusion

MOTH

MYSTERY, CONCEALMENT, ILLUSION

CARD MEANING: While some species of moth are diurnal, we tend to associate moths with the night. Moths are beautiful night pollinators, doing important work under the cover of darkness. Moths are often compelled to seek out the light, even though it may endanger them.

Moths, like butterflies, often have markings that disguise them, tricking predators into assuming they are something other than what they truly are. This illusion serves as protection.

The Moth card tells you that perhaps something around you isn't what it seems. Look for the truth and follow the light, but don't let yourself be blinded. There may be something in your life that needs illumination in order for you to take control.

REFLECTION

What in your life needs illumination to enable you to see past a surface-level illusion?

MUSHROOM

Recycling, breaking down problems

MUSHROOM

RECYCLING, BREAKING DOWN PROBLEMS

CARD MEANING: A mushroom's main purpose is to aid in decomposition. They use enzymes to break down decaying organic matter, feeding themselves in the process. Mushrooms and other fungi are also part of the greater mycelial network, a vast interconnected network of hairlike roots that transfers information to not only other fungi, but plants and trees as well.

The Mushroom card supports you as you break down problems into smaller issues and work to solve them separately to make incremental advances in life. The discoveries you make with every step forward can be used to nourish and enrich future projects.

REFLECTION

Have you run into a challenge that may best be addressed if broken down into smaller pieces?

Sun

Healing energy, happiness, comfort, joy

48

SUN

HEALING ENERGY, HAPPINESS, COMFORT, JOY

CARD MEANING: The sun is the main source of life on our planet. It holds great power in the green witch practice. It gives us light, which feeds plant life and is essential to the process of photosynthesis. From these plants comes oxygen, nourishing us when we breathe.

Sunlight also brings comfort to our bodies, easing chills and dampness, helping us stay warm. The Sun card is associated with robust health and healing illnesses. The light chases away the darkness and encourages joy and happiness.

Let light in to illuminate dark corners in your life. Allow optimism into your heart to encourage you. There are bright times ahead.

REFLECTION

What needs healing in your life?
What needs comfort and attention?

MOON

Phases, cycles, intuition

MOON

PHASES, CYCLES, INTUITION

CARD MEANING: The pale glowing moon is visible at different degrees throughout its monthly cycle. Even though its appearance changes, the moon is always present. Take solace in knowing nature is always there for you.

The waxing and waning of the moon reminds you that nothing is static, and that change is both inevitable and healthy; you just may not be able to see it all the time. The phases of the moon represent various energies as manifested in the growth and retreat cycle of nature itself. Nothing is ever at a standstill in the natural world, and the same goes for the energy flowing inside you. Sometimes you may find you retreat into yourself, and other times, you reach outward for help. The Moon card asks you to trust what your intuition tells you to do.

REFLECTION

*Do you tend to withdraw when overwhelmed,
or do you reach out for help?*

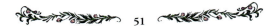

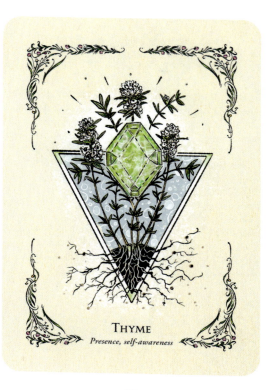

THYME

Presence, self-awareness

THYME

PRESENCE, SELF-AWARENESS

CARD MEANING: With its sharp scent, thyme tells you to be in the moment and pay attention to the state of your mind, body, and spirit. In green witchcraft, we rely on herbs to help ground us. The Thyme card is asking you to be present and self-aware. It may be time to take an inventory of how you feel. With all the pretense, wishful thinking, and illusion stripped away, evaluate yourself honestly. Take note of areas that sting or hurt, and what feels good.

Try not to judge your feelings. Just offer them love and understanding, and remember that feelings are not actions. It takes strength and effort to stay present in your life.

REFLECTION

Have you been fully present in your daily life? If not, what steps can you take to change this?

WATERING CAN

Asking for help, sharing burdens

WATERING CAN

ASKING FOR HELP, SHARING BURDENS

CARD MEANING: Not everything happens naturally. Sometimes you must carry water to a plant. Being a green witch means stepping up to honor nature and act on its behalf. Sometimes that manifests as giving a plant what it lacks so that it can thrive. The reciprocal relationship between you and nature means that sometimes you're the one who needs nature's help, and sometimes nature needs your help.

When you're lacking something, however, it can at first be hard to admit you need to ask for help. The Watering Can card tells you that something in your life needs external support, or that a burden needs to be shared. Don't be afraid to lean on others.

REFLECTION

Is there something in your life that needs outside attention, or an injection of energy from elsewhere?

BASIL

Prosperity, luck, love

BASIL

PROSPERITY, LUCK, LOVE

CARD MEANING: Basil is one of the most versatile herbs in a green witch's tool kit. Full of positive energy, it can draw good things into your life. Basil has been known to dispel fear, confusion, or any weakness, and was even used as an aromatic by ancient Greeks to attract love. In this way, basil is all about forward movement.

The Basil card tells you that the time is right for something that you may have been hesitant about in the past. The time for planning and preparing is over; go forth with confidence. It's an auspicious time. This is a great moment to indulge in love or take a risk. Basil has your back, and luck is on your side!

REFLECTION

Have you been scared to take a leap or risk that may pay off greatly?

CHAMOMILE

Gentleness, relaxation, sleep

CHAMOMILE

GENTLENESS, RELAXATION, SLEEP

CARD MEANING: With its gentle energy and flavor, chamomile suggests that perhaps you need to slow down a bit. There's something in your life that is draining you or wearing you down—a relationship, a situation—and the Chamomile card quietly reminds you that if you're in a state of exhaustion you won't be able to do the work that will be required in the future, either at all or to the extent you'll need to.

Chamomile invites you to take a pause. Step away from your work, whatever kind it may be, and give your mind, body, and spirit time to find balance and equilibrium.

REFLECTION

Have you struggled to give yourself permission to rest recently?

RAIN

Cleansing, purification, hydration

RAIN

CLEANSING, PURIFICATION, HYDRATION

CARD MEANING: Water is one of the essentials of life, and one of the four classical elements that we use in magical work. Rain hydrates soil and plants. It can be a gentle sprinkling to moisten your garden, or a heavy deluge, enough to wash away previously stable land.

The Rain card tells you that something in your life needs cleansing or purification. It may be a light cleansing, or it may be a full-on reshaping of your situation. There may be a part of your life that is parched and needs the rejuvenation. Meditate on the warning that this card brings, and use the energy of water to purify the imbalance. Let the rain wash away what overwhelms you.

REFLECTION

Is there a part of your life that is eroding due to an unceasing flow of unstable energy?

MINT
Abundance, persistence, proliferation

MINT

ABUNDANCE, PERSISTENCE, PROLIFERATION

CARD MEANING: The Mint card speaks of deep roots, firm grounding, and a refusal to give in. The tenacity of the mint herb can be the despair of many a gardener, but its abundance can also be an encouraging omen. Life's obstacles can be frustrating, but mint reminds you that stubbornness can get you through.

Consider your current situation. Someone may be trying to uproot you, or remove you from something you're passionate about. Don't let them. Make your own decisions and don't let someone else steal your agency. Dig in and be strong. Stubbornness isn't necessarily a negative trait!

REFLECTION

Are there unfair limitations being imposed on you by someone or something?

CUP OF TEA

Patience, reassessment

CUP OF TEA

PATIENCE, REASSESSMENT

CARD MEANING: A cup of tea provides you with a moment of quiet. Savor the process and stay present. This brewing takes time, just as a tricky situation takes time to develop. A quick reaction may not be the way to go. Have patience and let things ripen. Just as an infusion of herbs takes time to come to full potency, magical work rarely produces instantaneous results.

Remember: A watched pot never boils; let it do its work in its own time, and trust in your process. Use the time to reflect on the situation and how you feel about it, and reassess your perspective. The Cup of Tea card reminds you that perhaps all is not as it seems.

REFLECTION

Are there lessons you can learn from a difficult situation that you haven't considered yet?

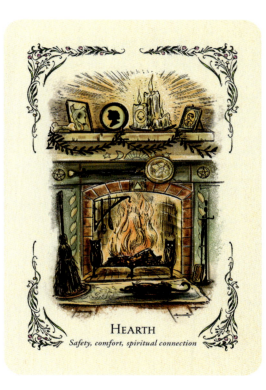

HEARTH

Safety, comfort, spiritual connection

HEARTH

SAFETY, COMFORT, SPIRITUAL CONNECTION

CARD MEANING: The hearth is the spiritual heart of your home, symbolizing the presence of Spirit. A physical hearth provides light, warmth, and a way to prepare nourishment. The spiritual hearth represents the spiritual nature of the home, the essence of what makes it a place of rest, rejuvenation, and comfort. The location of the spiritual hearth is unimportant, as is whatever you might use or recognize as its physical representation. It may be a feeling, a meditation, a blanket.

Hearth also symbolizes connection with those you consider family, as well as Spirit. This card suggests that you look to those relationships and do what is necessary to reinforce them. Renew your connection to your hearth to keep the communication with Spirit in your home vibrant.

REFLECTION

In what way does your connection to Spirit need attention?

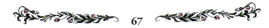

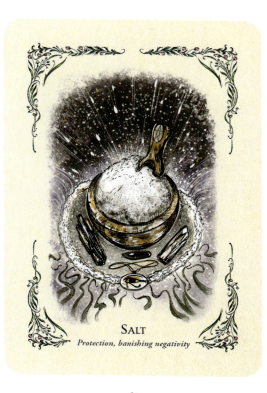

SALT

Protection, banishing negativity

Salt

PROTECTION, BANISHING NEGATIVITY

CARD MEANING: Salt is essential to life. This mineral is so precious that it has been used as currency at times in history when its collection was labor-intensive and time-consuming. In magic, it is an all-purpose component, used to create barriers to protect you, as a purifying ingredient in various blessing or holy waters, and as a cleansing implement that removes unwanted energy from magical tools or spaces.

The Salt card reminds you that you have easy means to dispel negativity and protect yourself. You don't have to struggle! Salt is your partner in self-defense. Draw boundaries and keep yourself guarded against negativity. Remember to keep the energy surrounding you as clean as possible.

REFLECTION

Is there someone or something you need to set a boundary with for your own well-being?

MORTAR AND PESTLE

Integration, subtlety, thoroughness

Mortar and Pestle

INTEGRATION, SUBTLETY, THOROUGHNESS

CARD MEANING: The goals of the mortar and pestle are twofold: first to reduce the size of something, and then to combine ingredients. In a spell, in order to evenly combine your components, you need to break them down into smaller parts. The grinding motion used with a mortar and pestle can appear aggressive, and applying too much force can make your ingredients fly everywhere. Use finesse. Be gentle but thorough. Take the time to blend things evenly.

This card tells you that something in your life needs to be better incorporated. It could be as simple as integrating your practice into daily life, or something more complex, like finding balance between two relationships. Whatever it is, take it slow or you'll scatter what you're trying to integrate.

REFLECTION

*What parts of your life do you need
to blend more seamlessly?*

BEE

Community, cooperation, sweetness

Bee

COMMUNITY, COOPERATION, SWEETNESS

CARD MEANING: Bees inspire thoughts of sweetness and community. Bees work together, functioning in cooperation with others to advance the health and safety of their entire hive. Communication is central to this goal. In the end, through hard work and service to others, they create something pure and sweet: honey. It's the sweetness of honey that reminds us to be kind to others.

The Bee card asks you to consider if you feel fulfilled and connected in your relationships, or if you need to communicate your needs to others more. Remember to be kind whenever you can, and to meet any challenge with an open heart.

REFLECTION

What part of your life needs clearer communication? How can you work more effectively with others?

BUTTERFLY
Transformation, joy, beauty, transience

BUTTERFLY

TRANSFORMATION, JOY, BEAUTY, TRANSIENCE

CARD MEANING: Butterflies are commonly associated with beauty and joy. They are inspirational in their loveliness, but the journey they go through to achieve this metamorphosis is even more inspirational, if less pretty. Caterpillars must completely dissolve in the chrysalis, giving up their very physical selves in the process of transformation. Only once they have relinquished everything can their physical matter be reassembled as butterflies.

The idea of that much sacrifice can be overwhelming, even if the end result is glorious. Fear of change can also hold you back. Let the beauty and joy that await you inspire courage. Trust that achieving your goal will be worth it. The Butterfly card urges you not to be afraid to let yourself grow and become something new!

REFLECTION

Are you afraid to make a change, especially if this change means giving up parts of yourself in the process?

BIRD

Freedom, opportunity

BIRD

FREEDOM, OPPORTUNITY

CARD MEANING: As symbols of freedom in many cultures, birds tell us that we, too, can soar. Conversely, many bird species are tied to a food source in a specific region, so they are completely interconnected with local land and its energies. Finding a balance between these two extremes can be challenging.

Migration is another challenge. There is an element of sacrifice involved in leaving the known and familiar, and trusting in your intuition to get to where you need to be.

The Bird card also tells you that a new opportunity is close by. Lift your head past your current focus and look around for it. A bird's-eye view may reveal something you might otherwise have never known about. New opportunities are on the horizon.

REFLECTION

Have you been struggling to change your mindset and learn something new?

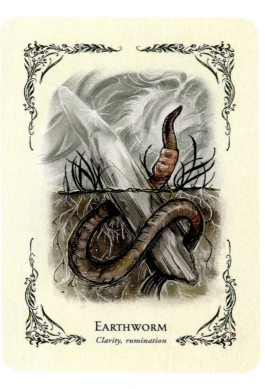

EARTHWORM

Clarity, rumination

EARTHWORM

CLARITY, RUMINATION

CARD MEANING: The humble earthworm breaks down organic material and aerates soil, serving an essential function in the health of plants. Without the earthworm's work, the soil would be too heavy and lack the oxygen roots need to thrive. Additionally, the organic matter wouldn't be as well blended in the soil.

The Earthworm card reminds you that some essential work is happening under the surface in your life. Nature is bringing you closer to your goal. It also suggests that it's time to confront what troubles you. Consider breaking down big emotions into less-intimidating smaller chunks that are easier to digest and understand.

REFLECTION

What can you do to help yourself when you feel overwhelmed?

HEDGE
Potential, boundaries, indecision

HEDGE

POTENTIAL, BOUNDARIES, INDECISION

CARD MEANING: The hedge, or natural boundary, serves two purposes: to define a safe zone, protecting you from what's outside, or to keep you in one place, like a pen. The Hedge card asks you to review your own boundaries and how you respond to boundaries created by others.

A hedge is also a symbol of moving between two states of being, or two worlds. "Riding the hedge" is a phrase used to describe spirit journeys where a witch's awareness travels to acquire information and undertake new experiences. The hedge belongs to neither world, being the liminal space between the two. If you are in that liminal space, it's time to choose which side to step into for now. You can't stay there forever.

REFLECTION

Do you need to be firmer about how you allow others to impact you, or are your boundaries so strong that you push people away?

OAK TREE

Power, courage, strength

OAK TREE

POWER, COURAGE, STRENGTH

CARD MEANING: The oak tree is a popular symbol of strength. The wood is dense and durable, reliable, and long-lasting. This tree symbolizes power and bravery, telling you that you can stand up to whatever storm is on the horizon.

The mighty oak begins as a tiny acorn. It is reassuring to know that something so immense and strong started out as something that you can hold between two fingers. Not only does it remind us that small things can yield huge results, it also reminds us that growing takes time. Rapid growth uses energy to reach a goal quickly. Slow growth uses energy to ensure stable, strong development. The Oak Tree card urges you to be brave and to stand tall.

REFLECTION

Is there something you've been avoiding because of the fear of confrontation?

PINE TREE
Vitality, longevity, perseverance

84

PINE TREE

VITALITY, LONGEVITY, PERSEVERANCE

CARD MEANING: The pine tree is a symbol of life enduring, the promise that even if things seem dark, it's not over. Some kinds of pine trees have root systems that are centuries old, and while a single tree may die, the established root system can introduce a new seedling to replace it. The rejuvenation cycle tells us that even when something appears to be dead or finished, there are still roots alive. Nothing is ever truly gone. Don't give up on it.

Pine is a popular building material. It absorbs shock, is resistant to excessive swelling and shrinking, and although it dents easily, it is long-lasting. The Pine Tree card tells you to hang in there. Life may be knocking you around a bit, but even dented, you're reliable and can last longer than you think.

REFLECTION

Have you given up on something you shouldn't have?

Preserve

Security, forethought, thrift

PRESERVE

SECURITY, FORETHOUGHT, THRIFT

CARD MEANING: In green witchcraft, preserving a harvest allows you to keep it longer, instead of losing it to decay or waste. It's a thrifty measure that enables you to rely on the fruits of your labor for an extended period of time.

Another form of preserving is to put aside a little of what you use every time you use it. This helps build a stockpile to guard against future need. This process is an ongoing low-level investment that doesn't take much time or energy.

The Preserve card reminds you that small gestures accumulate over time. Keep an eye out for areas where you can be thrifty with your time and energy. This doesn't mean you have to deprive yourself now. Enjoy your harvest, just don't use it all at once simply because it's there.

> **REFLECTION**
>
> *How can you work to store and secure
> what you have successfully produced?*

WALKING STAFF

Support, encouragement

WALKING STAFF

SUPPORT, ENCOURAGEMENT

CARD MEANING: The walking staff is as at home providing help and support when you are tromping through the woods, as it is comfortable in a garden being used to prop something up. In essence, the staff is a form of wand, a magical tool used to direct energy and aid in focus.

The Walking Staff card suggests that some part of your life needs more support, something to lean on, or something to help you focus your efforts. Like a plant may need a stake to help it stay upright until it develops enough strength in its stem to stand alone, your life may be easier if you have something or someone to lean on. A journey can take much less effort if you use a walking staff to give you extra security along the way.

REFLECTION

*Can you identify which parts of your life
are lacking strength?*

ROSEMARY

Remembrance, loyalty, faithfulness

ROSEMARY

REMEMBRANCE, LOYALTY, FAITHFULNESS

CARD MEANING: Rosemary is an aromatic herb closely associated with loyalty, devotion, and remembrance of the dead. The sharp, piney smell is clean, helping to clear away confusion and uncertainty. Rosemary's needles grow on woody stems, a strong core that is not easily broken.

The Rosemary card tells you to be faithful to what you hold sacred in your life. Whether that is your values, beliefs, people, or whatever you feel passionate about, remember these things and honor them. Keep them in mind when making choices. Don't let the world sway you from your ideals.

REFLECTION

What do you hold to be sacred in your life?

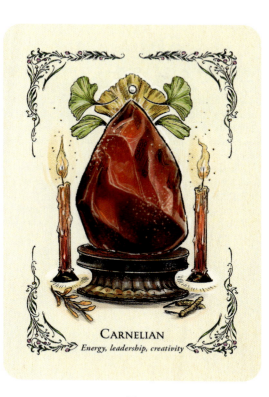

CARNELIAN

Energy, leadership, creativity

CARNELIAN

ENERGY, LEADERSHIP, CREATIVITY

CARD MEANING: Carnelian is associated with creativity and energy, two elements that enhance leadership. Carnelian can strengthen your leadership qualities and help you find creative solutions to problems or ways to support your team. If you have to take the lead in something or are handed a situation that needs a firm hand, carnelian can give you the confidence to do what needs to be done, even if it will make waves.

Carnelian's orange color comes from iron oxide, so it carries iron associations as well, such as protection and courage. The Carnelian card tells you to take control and be brave. Look within for motivation and strength. You have what it takes to be a leader. Be confident in your abilities.

REFLECTION

How can you improve your leadership skills?

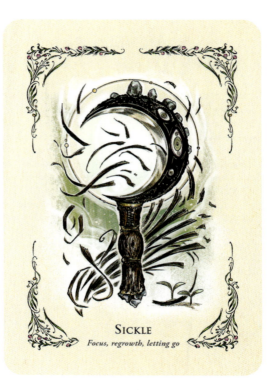

SICKLE

Focus, regrowth, letting go

SICKLE

FOCUS, REGROWTH, LETTING GO

CARD MEANING: The sickle is a gardening tool used for harvesting and reaping, though it is also closely associated with death. In art, Death is often seen holding this tool, a symbol of taking a life that has finished.

The sickle helps you to clear away dead matter and control overgrowth, allowing for new growth to take place unhindered. Clearing and cutting away outdated or unneeded material leaves space for new life and beginnings. It doesn't cut life short. Instead, it refocuses available resources so that life can continue. The Sickle card reminds you to cut away what drains your energy or no longer serves you so focused growth can take place.

REFLECTION

What parts of your life need to be cut back or cut out completely to help you grow?

SEEDS

New ideas, hope, open-mindedness

SEEDS

NEW IDEAS, HOPE, OPEN-MINDEDNESS

CARD MEANING: A seed contains the blueprint for an entirely new plant, a future living thing. It is a miracle that something so small holds the key to new life.

There is so much potential within a seed. In fact, planting a seed is an act of hope. It's the first step in a project or undertaking, trusting that in the future you will actualize your dream. However, there's work ahead. If the seed sprouts, it will need care and attention to maximize its potential. You will need to nourish it to help it grow.

The Seeds card tells you that there is something worth your time that is waiting to be recognized. Be open to the messages nature has for you. Don't immediately dismiss ideas as far-fetched or impossible. Give them consideration. There may be something to learn.

REFLECTION

When you are thinking about new ideas or new projects, what do you want to achieve?

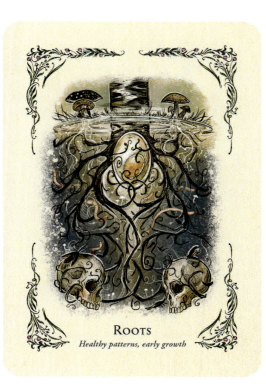

Roots

Healthy patterns, early growth

ROOTS

HEALTHY PATTERNS, EARLY GROWTH

CARD MEANING: Roots create a foundation, giving a plant stability and strength. Twining deep throughout the soil, they are both anchors and explorers, seeking water and nutrients to feed the plant. Roots expand and divide, creating beautiful natural patterns.

The Roots card reminds you to make sure your project has good roots. Don't race through this early stage of creation. If you ensure a healthy foundation in the early stages, your project will have a better chance of success.

Like a strong root system that will support and nourish a plant, it's important to establish routines and healthy patterns you can rely on when life gets chaotic. A reliable foundation will bring you confidence and reduce pressure in times of stress.

REFLECTION

Do you need to go back to the foundations of something to examine them and perhaps reinforce them?

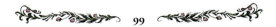

TRUNK

Stability, loyalty, reliability

TRUNK

STABILITY, LOYALTY, RELIABILITY

CARD MEANING: Like a spine, the stalk or trunk is the central column of a plant from which everything branches. It is both the support and connector, unifying the extremities of crown and roots. The newer, softer wood just beneath the protective bark of the trunk conveys moisture from the ground upward, and moves energy created in the leaves downward. The core is what gives the tree its strength.

Like a tree, your core has been formed of past experiences as you've grown. Make a list of your core beliefs—who you are, what you hold dear, and what you would never compromise on. This is who you truly are. The Trunk card reminds you to stay true to those beliefs to provide a safe, stable place for new experiences to develop.

REFLECTION

What have some formative experiences in your life been and how have they shaped who you are today?

LEAVES

Renewal, revival, progress

LEAVES

RENEWAL, REVIVAL, PROGRESS

CARD MEANING: Leaves are how plants and trees take in sunlight, and, as part of photosynthesis, convert it into food. The process also transforms carbon dioxide into oxygen, a by-product that further sustains much of non-plant life on earth. In this way, the Leaves card reminds you that you may need to pull ideas and solutions from different places to get your desired results. Don't just rely on well-used patterns. Work to merge new patterns into your life.

Leaves grow every year on deciduous trees, reminding us that cycles continue and that the energy of nature revives after its fallow period. Leaves are how a tree interacts and communicates with its environment. Pay attention to leaves and you likely will find you are more in touch with the weather, seasonal shifts, and the well-being of your immediate environment.

> ### REFLECTION
>
> *Do you need to pay more attention to*
> *your feelings and intuition?*

BUDS
New beginnings, expansion

BUDS

NEW BEGINNINGS, EXPANSION

CARD MEANING: A bud is one of the earliest visual confirmations that the seed you planted is hard at work. Whether a budding leaf or bloom, it's proof that your endeavor is in motion. So far, so good!

Buds are tender, delicate things, however, which still need close attention and care. Extreme weather can damage them, as can neglect. The Buds card shows that you can interpret the success of this first stage as a positive sign, but don't assume the buds can handle the next stages on their own.

Buds represent the first checkpoint in a project. Things are expanding, but not complete. Continue to tend and encourage them, as without buds, there can be no fruit. Have confidence. The success of your first stage promises that you can achieve your goal!

REFLECTION

Are there things in your life that you've left unfinished or abandoned? How can you help complete them?

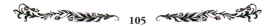

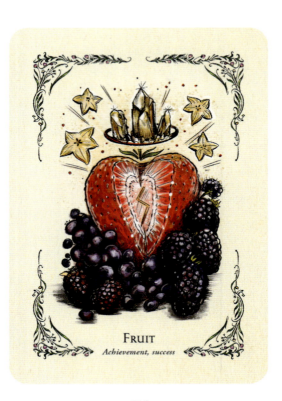

Fruit

Achievement, success

FRUIT

ACHIEVEMENT, SUCCESS

CARD MEANING: Fruit is tangible proof of an achievement. When we say that something has "borne fruit," we mean it has been successful. In this way, the Fruit card tells you that all your hard work has yielded a satisfying result, or is about to produce a wonderful result. Be proud of your efforts.

Producing something—a project, an object, a baby—takes time, energy, and attention. And sometimes work can be invisible to others, happening behind the scenes or internally. The fruit of that labor, however, is proof that energy was invested. Recognize and honor it.

Fruit also tells you that you can catch your breath for a bit. Celebrate your success!

REFLECTION

Have you been working too hard on something and need a break?

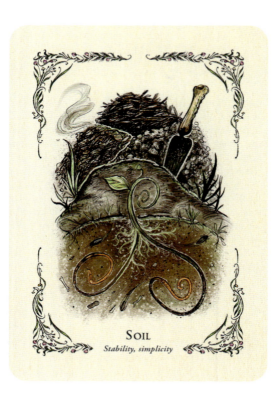

Soil

Stability, simplicity

SOIL

STABILITY, SIMPLICITY

CARD MEANING: Just because something is simple doesn't mean it's easy. Soil is a basic part of a garden, and it seems pretty straightforward, but there's a complicated community of microbes and a balance of minerals and elements required for it to successfully support life. It's easy to remember to tend growing plants, but you also need to tend the health of the soil as well. It is the basis of your garden and provides stability and insulation, as well as a varied source of nutrients plants need to thrive.

Soil is the ground under your feet, offering reassurance; the Soil card reminds you that it's always there for you. But don't forget to check your connection to that foundation, and don't turn your back on the basics.

REFLECTION

Are you overcomplicating or overthinking something that is actually quite simple?

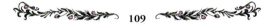

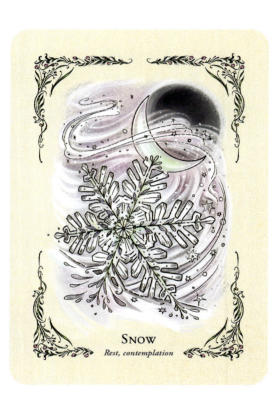

SNOW

Rest, contemplation

SNOW

REST, CONTEMPLATION

CARD MEANING: Snow plays a variety of roles in the winter season. In a garden, snow adds nutrients, elements, and moisture to the soil. It also acts as an insulator, keeping the ground and plants protected from major temperature fluctuations.

The peace of a snowfall invites you to release the stress you've been carrying. But snow isn't always peaceful. Snowstorms force you to sit still, shutting down activity and travel. Without your typical choices, storms force you to confront what you might have been avoiding.

The Snow card asks you to reflect on the past. Time gives you a clearer head with which to review these events. Snow can help you work through your emotions and see the past in a more balanced fashion. Trust what may seem like a slowdown, because it could be exactly what you need to stay safe.

REFLECTION

What good things can you carry forward in life?
What can you release?

FOG

Obscurity, feeling lost

Fog

OBSCURITY, FEELING LOST

CARD MEANING: Sometimes, for whatever reason, you can't see clearly. You find it difficult to think through an issue or you feel lost in a sea of information. You may feel directionless, or unable to identify a clear goal or path to a desired outcome. Being lost in fog or feeling foggy can challenge your sense of stability.

Fog isn't a solid obstacle, however. It's like a veil, temporarily blurring your surroundings. Just because you can't see clearly doesn't mean the path isn't there. Carefully feel your way forward one step at a time. Perhaps you need to move in a different direction to reach your destination. Sometimes all it takes is looking at a problem in a new way. The Fog card prompts you to practice looking at things from other points of view.

REFLECTION

Do you have a problem plaguing you that could benefit from a different perspective?

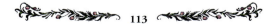

SPRING

Rebuilding, awakening, rebirth

SPRING

REBUILDING, AWAKENING, REBIRTH

CARD MEANING: The reawakening of the earth is always inspiring. New life is on the horizon! It can be invigorating to witness the stirring of energy after a long rest.

Spring tells you that it's time for new beginnings. It's the perfect time to launch a new project, or, if there are things you previously put on hold, the Spring card suggests that now is an auspicious time to revisit them. You will bring a refreshed perspective to this project, and a new level of energy that you didn't have before. Perhaps all that was needed was a new approach after some time away and a new burst of motivation and determination.

REFLECTION

Is there a project you want to launch that you've previously ignored?

SUMMER

Expansion, growth

SUMMER

EXPANSION, GROWTH

CARD MEANING: Summer is bursting with energy. The sun is high, the weather is warmer, and the nights are shorter. Summer brings increased growth for all living things. But all this energy and unrestricted growth can get out of hand. Increased growth means increased attention is required to manage your projects so you ensure everything unfolds properly.

The Summer card means it's an optimal time for expansion, but it also tells you to keep an eye on the energies in your life so that they stay focused and productive. If you don't tend your garden, it will become overgrown and scraggly. Some endeavors will fail as others overshadow them, like a vine strangling a beautiful plant.

REFLECTION

What parts of your life can you expand to feel more fulfilled?

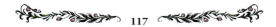

Autumn

Bounty, balance

Autumn

BOUNTY, BALANCE

CARD MEANING: Autumn is a time to slow down. The high energy of summer's expansion calms and turns to a slower rhythm. There is space for acknowledgment and gratitude, as the intense production of the previous season yields a crop.

The autumn equinox is a time of balance, when the hours of daylight and night are equal. The Autumn card reminds you that balance is important, whether it means balancing work with appreciation for the harvest, or balancing intake and output of energy. Don't overtax yourself. Remember to refuel in times of hard work.

REFLECTION

Have you been successful when it comes to balancing your work and personal life? If not, how can you strike a better balance?

WINTER
An ending, recharging, reflection

WINTER

AN ENDING, RECHARGING, REFLECTION

CARD MEANING: Winter is a quiet time. In nature, most plant life is suspended, animals are hibernating, and food becomes scarce. Winter tells you that the end of something is coming, or has already happened. Don't lament. This also means there is an opportunity for something new and better. In every end there is a beginning. The cycle of nature never stops.

The Winter card encourages rest and reflection on what has come to be. Mourn if you need to. Identify the things that went well and what you want to do differently. As you engage in this reflection, remember to look ahead to spring, and begin to consider what projects you'd like to focus on next using the knowledge you've gained from this time of assessment.

REFLECTION

What big lessons have you learned after slowing down and allowing yourself time to reflect on what has ended or passed?

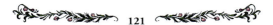

Sow

Planning, setting intentions, optimism

Sow

PLANNING, SETTING INTENTIONS, OPTIMISM

CARD MEANING: Seeds may be the nebulous concept, and soil the fertile ground to nourish them, but the act of sowing is what unites the two and initializes the process of germination. When you sow seeds, you scatter them in or on the earth, asking the soil to help them grow. For a time, the seeds have to remain quiet underground before they can launch into the world. This dormancy allows them the opportunity to gather strength.

The Sow card tells you that now is the optimal time to set things in motion. Plant your seeds and nurture them. Lock in your intentions and take the first steps along the path you've planned. Act now for future yield. Prime your material and environment for the best outcome. If you've been hesitating, now is the time to act.

REFLECTION

Are you ready to start something new?

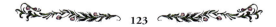

TEND

Maintenance, encouragement, guidance

TEND

MAINTENANCE, ENCOURAGEMENT, GUIDANCE

CARD MEANING: Tending your garden is an important step in creating a thriving ecosystem. Maintaining a garden means weeding, snipping away dead flowers and leaves, fertilizing, and pinching back overgrowth to redirect energy—it's a cooperative experience.

The Tend card is a reminder that you, too, deserve maintenance. It's important to review the different parts of your life every once in a while with a keen eye, looking for areas you can tend for positive results. Just as you guide your garden, your energy also deserves loving guidance and encouragement.

You may need to weed toxicity out of your life. Be discerning about where you put your energy. Ask for guidance and listen to the messages Spirit sends you.

REFLECTION

What areas of your life need support?
What areas are threatened by toxicity?

HARVEST

Determination, hard work

Harvest

Determination, hard work

CARD MEANING: Harvest time means hard work. It's time to reap the results of sowing and tending, and that usually means a lot of effort concentrated in a short period of time. This time can be just as exhausting as when you sowed your seeds, but it is a necessary part of the successful growing season.

Sometimes you might think that it's all about sitting back and enjoying the fruits of your labor. It's important to appreciate your success, but don't lose your way. The Harvest card directs you to collect your bounty, to recognize your blessings, and to not stop working too early. You're almost there, but you still have things to see through. Work to recoup the energy you previously invested.

REFLECTION

Are you burning out because of too much hard work too quickly? How can you give yourself support as you reap the bounty of your efforts?

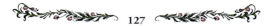

Index of Oracle Cards